12 THINGS TO KNOW ABOUT

THE NEOLITHIC ERA

by Meg Marquardt

12 STORY LIBRARY
MORE TO EXPLORE

www.12StoryLibrary.com

12-Story Library is an imprint of Bookstaves.

Photographs ©: Osama Shukir Muhammed Amin FRCP(Glasg)/CC4.0, cover, 1; Morphart Creation/Shutterstock.com, 4; Omar hoftun/CC3.0, 5; PHGCOM/CC3.0, 6; Zde/CC4.0, 7; Pikoso.kz/Shutterstock.com, 8; HTO/PD, 9; Cristian Chirita/CC3.0, 10; Purchase, Colt Archaeological Institute Inc. Gift, 1983/PD, 11; Kritheus/CC4.0, 12; Elelicht/CC3.0, 13; Dr._Colleen_Morgan/CC2.0, 15; Einsamer Schütze/CC4.0, 16; English Heritage/Alamy, 17; Nevit Dilmen/CC3.0, 18; Erkcan/PD, 19; Marie-Lan Nguyen/PD, 20; Rezso Lázár/CC3.0, 21; James William Smith/Shutterstock.com, 22; Hussein shejaeya/CC4.0, 23; MNStudio/Shutterstock.com, 24; Wolfgang Sauber/CC3.0, 25; PD, 26; Faces of Ancient Europe/YouTube, 27; JMiall/CC3.0, 29

ISBN
9781632357700 (hardcover)
9781632358790 (paperback)
9781645820512 (ebook)

Library of Congress Control Number: 2019938690

Printed in the United States of America
July 2019

About the Cover

A Halaf pottery jar discovered in Mesopotamia from the Neolithic Age.

Access free, up-to-date content on this topic plus a full digital version of this book. Scan the QR code on page 31 or use your school's login at 12StoryLibrary.com.

Table of Contents

1

Neolithic People Started the Agricultural Revolution

The ground was fresh. No one had ever farmed it before. That's because farming was a brand-new invention. No one had ever done it before. Now, though, a small group of humans put seeds into the earth. They planted them where the sun would shine. They gave them water. The grains grew tall and healthy. Then the people harvested the grains, storing them indoors for winter. The agricultural revolution had begun.

The agricultural revolution is also known as the Neolithic Revolution. The Neolithic era is the third and final part of the Stone Age. It stretches from around 9,000 years ago to 4,000 years ago. This 5,000-year span is the last when humans will use stone tools. After this, they will jump to using metal tools.

But before that jump, humans have a lot of growing to do. This happens at different times in different places. The start of the Neolithic era is marked by farming. But farming didn't pop up at the same time all over the world. The farming revolution started around 9,000

Çatalhöyük after the first excavations.

years ago in Asia and the Middle East. It didn't start in Europe until around 8,000 years ago.

Farming opened up a lot of possibilities. People could stay in one place and build. Societies grew larger. Life started to look more like modern-day living.

9,500

Age in years of Çatalhöyük, a Neolithic city in south-central Turkey

- Çatalhöyük (chah-tahl-HU-yook) was discovered in 1958.
- It is one of the world's most important archaeological sites.
- People lived there for 2,000 years.

TIMING ISSUES

In the late 1800s, Danish archaeologist C.J. Thompsen came up with the three-age system. He split humankind's past into the Stone, Bronze, and Iron ages. Later, the Stone Age was divided into the Paleolithic, Mesolithic, and Neolithic eras. Researchers now know there is a lot of overlap among the ages and eras. In some places, farming started as early as 12,000 years ago. But most societies didn't start farming until around 9,000 years ago.

2

Plants Were Domesticated

All plants used to be wild. That is hard to imagine in the modern era. But there were once no farms or even gardens. People foraged. They walked around and found wild plants to eat.

In Neolithic times, that all changed. Plants were domesticated. This means they were planted on purpose, grown, and harvested. Neolithic people had to invent tools to do the job. To plant rows of crops, they needed a hoe to dig up the earth. A hoe can be as simple as a stick. More advanced hoes have a stone tip.

This more advanced hoe has a stone tip.

Different sorts of plants were domesticated in different regions. People in Mexico planted squash and corn-like plants. In China, they grew rice and millet. In the Middle East, they planted fig trees.

6–10 million

Number of people alive before the farming revolution

- The world could only support that many foragers.
- It takes farming techniques to feed a larger population.
- Ten thousand years later, the world population would be 250 million.

A rough sandstone grain crusher from the Neolithic Age.

Tools found in ancient houses are a sign that Neolithic people were farming. Most grains can't be eaten whole. They are often covered in a hard shell or have other inedible parts. Archaeologists have found tools for grinding grains in Neolithic homes.

CLUES IN JEWELRY

Researchers use a lot of different techniques to understand the past. They know that hunters and farmers wore different types of jewelry. Early farmers wore beads and bracelets. Hunters wore shells. Researchers trace the spread of farming by looking for the spread of beads.

3 Animals Were Domesticated

Cows, sheep, and horses were all once wild. During the Neolithic era, humans started to domesticate them. Domestication is the process of taming an animal. A wolf is wild. But a dog is tame. A dog can be kept on a farm or even in the house. A wolf needs to stay in the wild.

The process of domestication takes a while. Early people would capture wild animals first. Then they would breed them. The offspring of those animals would grow up close to humans. Then people would breed the offspring. After a few generations, the animals would no longer be wild.

Animal domestication spread through trade and migration. Some cultures were creating cities and staying in one place. But people still moved around. Some migrated from settlement to settlement. Or they just decided to go someplace new.

Ancient petroglyphs indicate people moved with their animals.

Neolithic pigs' teeth were smaller, indicating domestication.

They might bring along a tame cow or sheep. Then people in the new location could learn how to domesticate animals, too.

10,000–10,400
Age in years of pig bones found in southeastern Turkey

- The bones were found at a site called Hallan Çemi.
- Archaeologists found many pig bones there.
- They think pigs might be the first animals people domesticated for food.

PROOF IN PIGS' TEETH

Archaeologists who studied pig bones at Hallan Çemi looked closely at the teeth. The molars were smaller than wild boar molars. This told the researchers that Neolithic people were changing wild boars into pigs by breeding. The researchers found more bones from young male pigs than female pigs. This meant the people were eating more male pigs. They were keeping the female pigs alive for breeding.

4 Pottery Production Boomed

Pottery is something else that sets Neolithic life apart. Before the Neolithic era, some pottery was made. It was mostly for practical purposes, like storing grain. But in the Neolithic era, pottery started to become art.

Fire is part of what changed pottery. Pottery is made of clay. The clay is shaped into objects. These objects are then put in a really hot oven. Neolithic villages built better ovens that could reach even higher temperatures. This allowed them to make different sorts of pottery.

For example, in China, people made ceramic pottery. This type uses high-quality clay. Some pieces were painted with animals or designs. Some had detailed carvings. They might be bowls or vases. They were still used for storage, too.

Pottery is such an important part of Neolithic life that archaeologists break up the period according to different types of pottery. If a new Neolithic site is discovered, they look for pottery. The type of pottery lets them know why someone might have lived at that site.

A pot from 6000 BCE.

A fragment of a Halaf bowl from 5600–5000 BCE, where different colors of paint are visible.

HALAF POTTERY

One of the best-known pottery cultures was the Halaf. The Halaf potters lived in Mesopotamia. This historical region covered much of Western Asia. Halaf pottery was special because it was polychromatic. This means the potters used different colors of paint on a single piece of pottery. The colors might be reds, browns, or blacks. Their work was elaborate. Paintings might be geometric patterns or highly detailed animals.

20,000

Age in years of the oldest known pieces of pottery

- They were found in Xianrendong Cave in southern China.
- People in China were making pottery long before other parts of the world.
- This pottery was probably used for cooking food.

5 Towns and Cities Were Built

The Neolithic settlement of Sesklo was discovered in the 1800s.

The rise of farming also meant the rise of settlements. A big part of having a village is having food around. Farming didn't just let people grow more food. It also let them store food. Stored food is a safety net. If there is a bad crop year or animals are scarce, people won't starve. Farming made it possible for people to stay in place, build a life, and form communities.

Sesklo is an example of an early Neolithic town. Sesklo is in Greece. Around 7,000 years ago, about 3,000 people lived there. They had potters' shops and homes made of mud brick. Their homes likely had windows and doors.

Because no one was around to record Neolithic history in writing, it's hard to know how the people of Sesklo lived. But the way they stored grain gives us a snapshot of their lives. Archaeologists found that the grain wasn't stored in people's homes. Instead, it was stored in a central place. This means the villagers worked together. They collected their harvests in one location to share with each other.

0

Streets and sidewalks in Çatalhöyük in south-central Turkey

- About 8,000 people lived in 2,000 houses that were all crammed together.
- To get in and out of their houses, they went through holes in the roofs.
- Archaeologists think the people of Çatalhöyük ate together on their rooftops.

THINK ABOUT IT

The people of Çatalhöyük filled their homes with paintings and sculptures. Why do you think they did that?

A reconstruction of the typical house in Çatalhöyük. People would enter by climbing down the ladder.

6

New Types of Social Structures Took Shape

Learning to farm meant more people could settle in the same place. In time, people came up with ways to grow even more food in the same amount of space. This is known as intensification. The population of the world began to rise. Societies became more complex. This brought new challenges for early humans.

One thing archaeologists look for is social stratification. Social standing is another way to put this. As societies form, people are divided into different social levels. Rich people have a higher social standing than poor people. People with certain kinds of jobs have a higher social standing than others. Understanding stratification helps scientists understand a society.

In Neolithic times, there wasn't money as we know it today. Stratification looked a little different. Researchers have found stratification in Neolithic graves. In some areas, farmers were buried in different ways. Some were buried with more tools than others. Maybe this meant they were more successful in life.

Another aspect of Neolithic life was specialization. Since there was enough food to go around, not everyone had to farm. People could be potters. They could weave fabric for clothing. Potters could trade pots for food.

20

Age in years of the world's first known plague victim

- She died in western Sweden approximately 5,000 years ago.
- The plague wiped out huge Neolithic farming communities. It caused large migrations.
- Living in bigger groups also increased the risk of disease.

Neolithic graves help archaeologists understand stratification.

THINK ABOUT IT

What would you like to specialize in, or be really good at? What will you need to learn so you can do that?

7

Fighting Grew More Intense

People who roam around don't belong to any particular place. But once people build homes and cities, the sense of belonging starts to grow. There is another side to this feeling. People already in a group might decide that other people don't belong. Or they might want something that another group has. Either can set the stage for fighting.

In 2006, archaeologists were called to a burial site in Germany. It contained 26 skeletons of adults and children. The skeletons were 7,000 years old. No one knows exactly what happened to them. But researchers think they got in a fight over limited resources in the area. All the remains belonged to the same group of early farmers. Another group nearby might have wanted their land. So they killed their neighbors and took it by force.

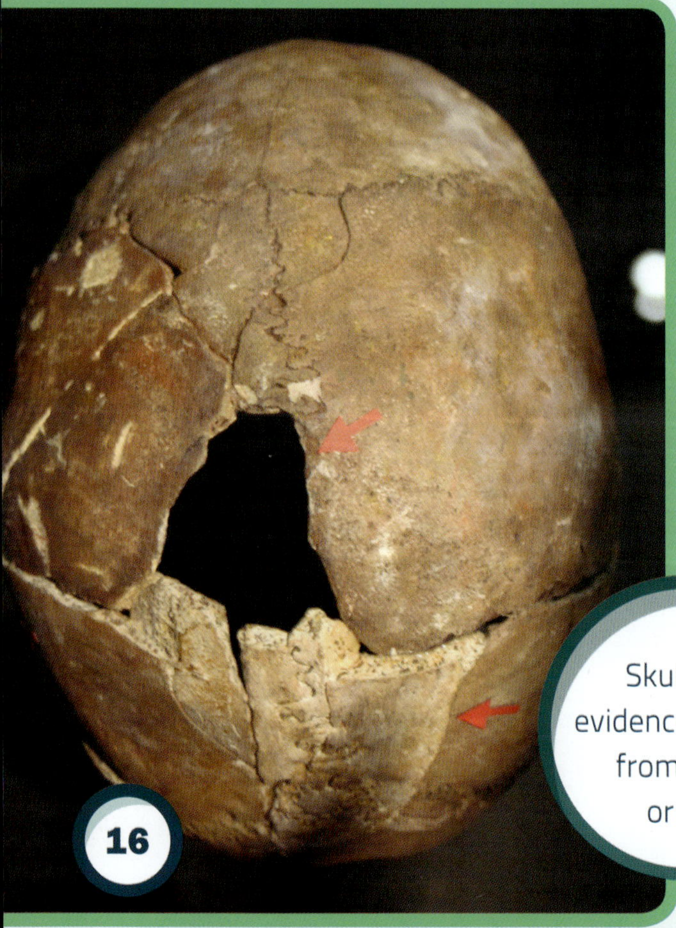

Skull with evidence of injury from a club or axe.

Archaeologists know fighting was involved by looking at the

WOMEN WERE STRONG

Bones can tell a little about how much muscle a person once had. Researchers looked at the bones of several Neolithic women. They found that these women were 30 percent stronger than the average woman today. This is probably because they were doing so much heavy lifting, like farming.

26 out of 350

Estimated number of Neolithic skulls that show traumatic injuries

- Archaeologists studied 350 skulls found in Neolithic graves.
- They found evidence of injuries by clubs, stone axes, and arrows. Some skulls still had bits of arrowheads in them.
- Maybe the Neolithic era wasn't as peaceful as some people think.

wounds on the skeletons. If someone dies of old age, their skeleton doesn't show much. But these skeletons have broken legs and bashed-in skulls. This tells the archaeologists that these people died a violent death.

8

Neolithic People Created Temples

Earlier humans moved around a lot. This meant only certain types of art were possible. People left paintings on cave walls and carved the occasional small statue out of rock. One benefit of staying put is the ability to devote more time to artistic projects and crafts.

Early people didn't stop anywhere long enough to build homes. So architecture came later than painting or sculpture. Once Neolithic people started building cities, they began to make buildings with style. Their temples are the earliest examples of religious architecture. These were large stone structures with complex interiors. They might have been used for worship. They could also have been used for trade and festivals.

The Seated Woman statue that was found in Turkey.

Most of the statues found at Çatalhöyük were animals.

One of the best-known examples of Neolithic art is a small statue known as the Seated Woman of Çatalhöyük. Found in Turkey, the statue is about four and a half inches (12 cm) tall. It is 9,000 years old. It was made of stones like marble, alabaster, and limestone. This shows that Neolithic artists were skilled at working with multiple materials. It's thought the Seated Woman was meant to represent a fertility goddess.

WOMEN AND MEN

Neolithic art often depicts women. Researchers wonder what this might mean in terms of gender roles. It could mean that some Neolithic people had a female goddess they worshiped. Researchers have also looked at bones. The bones suggest that women did similar jobs to men. Both bones and artwork could mean that men and women were considered equals. However, without more clues, we may never know for sure.

2,000

Number of carved figurines found at Çatalhöyük

- About 100 are statues of people.
- The other 1,900 are statues of animals.
- Çatalhöyük also has colorful murals painted on walls.

9

Neolithic People Had an Early Type of Writing

Only humans can write. But first, they had to invent writing. Early Neolithic people weren't exactly writing. But they were using symbols. This is called proto-writing. Proto-writing could be a collection of symbols, like a list. A farmer might make a list of the animals he owned. He would draw all his cows, sheep, and horses. He could use that list to show other people how many animals he had.

Neolithic people also invented a way to express numbers. They created small clay tokens. The tokens look like little seashells. They are different shapes and sizes. They might have holes or lines carved into

Clay tokens were used as a way to count things.

The three clay tablets were discovered in 1961.

them. Different shapes and designs might stand for different numbers. Archaeologists think these tokens were ways to count goods and keep track of them.

There are also disputed pieces of writing. For example, archaeologists found tortoise shells that had designs carved into them. Some researchers think the designs are a type of writing. Others aren't so sure. There are no other examples to compare the shells to. Without other instances, it's hard to tell if the shells really have writing on them. They could just be pretty designs.

THINK ABOUT IT

If you had to invent a new language, how would you start? Would you make up new letters or create a system that uses symbols?

3

Number of Neolithic tablets that might have writing on them

- The tablets were found in Romania.
- Scientists can't come to a consensus if the tablets contain writing or just symbols.
- There is also concern that the tablets could be fakes people are trying to pass off as real.

10

Jericho Was One of the First Great Cities

The Neolithic era was a time of great beginnings. One example is the city of Jericho. Jericho is in the West Bank, east of Israel and near the Jordan River. It is the oldest city in the world that people still live in today. It was founded 14,000 years ago.

It's not clear how many people lived in Jericho in Neolithic times. Some researchers say 300 people lived there. Others think it might have been as many as 3,000 people. There is evidence of early religion. Archaeologists have found human skulls with seashells in their eye sockets. It's not clear what the shells meant. But archaeologists think they were part of a ritual.

Ancient Jericho is best known for its famous walls. They were an early example of fortifications. These are structures built to keep a settlement safe. In this case, the walls were built

This stone tower unearthed by Kathleen Kenyon in Jericho helped date the city as the oldest in the world. The purpose of the tower is still unclear today.

Kenyon (right) and her assistant examine the Jericho skulls she discovered in 1953 that had seashells in their eye sockets.

20
Layers of settlements found in Jericho

- New settlements were built on top of old ones again and again, for many thousands of years.
- Jericho has survived floods, wars, and fires.
- In 2019, about 20,000 people were living in Jericho.

to keep out flooding from the Jordan River. They were built around 10,000 years ago and were 11.8 feet (3.6 meters) high. They would stand for more than 8,000 years.

Much of what we know about Jericho is because of Kathleen Kenyon. She was a British archaeologist who first came to Jericho in the 1950s. She was looking for the ruins of a Bronze Age city. What she found was much older. Her first finds went all the way back to the Neolithic era. If Kennedy hadn't come looking for ruins, people might never have known just how old Jericho is.

11

Neolithic People Made Mysterious Circular Enclosures

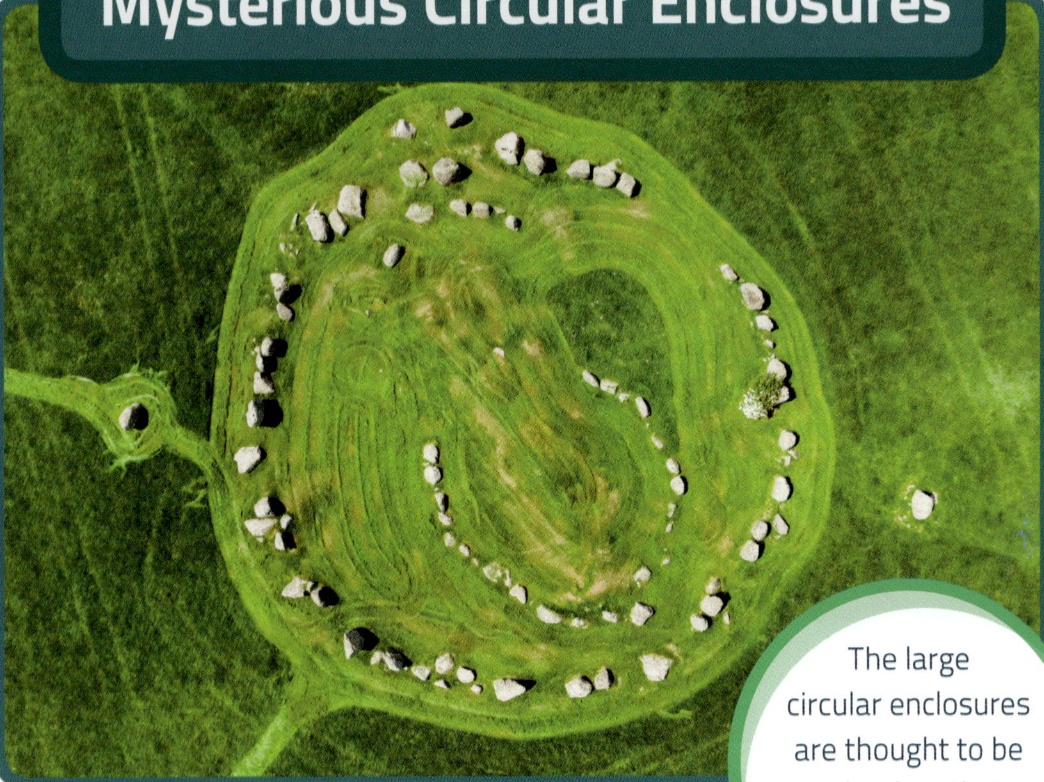

The large circular enclosures are thought to be calendars that track religious celebrations.

It's hard to say what Neolithic people might have believed in. There are some clues about religion, though. In central Europe, archaeologists have discovered large circular enclosures. These enclosures can be as big as 425 feet (130 m) in diameter. Some are so big their ruins can be seen from the sky.

The ruins of the enclosures are deep ditches. There are holes where wooden posts likely sat. An enclosure might be made up of multiple circles. Smaller circles would sit inside of larger ones. All the circles would be lined with posts. When the posts were up, an enclosure would have been sort of like a maze.

Researchers are fairly certain the enclosures had something to do with religion. There are specific places where the wooden posts would start and stop. The openings in between lined up with where the sun would be on a given date. Researchers think these enclosures were a type of calendar used to track religious celebrations.

One of the most famous enclosures is the Goseck circle in Germany. It was built around 6,900 years ago. It was last used about 6,700 years ago. Most enclosures were only around for that 200-year window. Researchers aren't sure why Neolithic people stopped building the enclosures. Maybe they had found another religion.

135

Number of circular enclosures discovered by 2011

- These are the oldest temple-like structures found in Europe.
- Some have two entrances. Others have as many as five.
- Because many of the enclosures are in Germany and Austria, researchers often call them by their German name, *Kreisgrabenanlagen*.

A circular enclosure was reconstructed in Germany to show the number of entrances.

12

Copper Put an End to the Stone Age

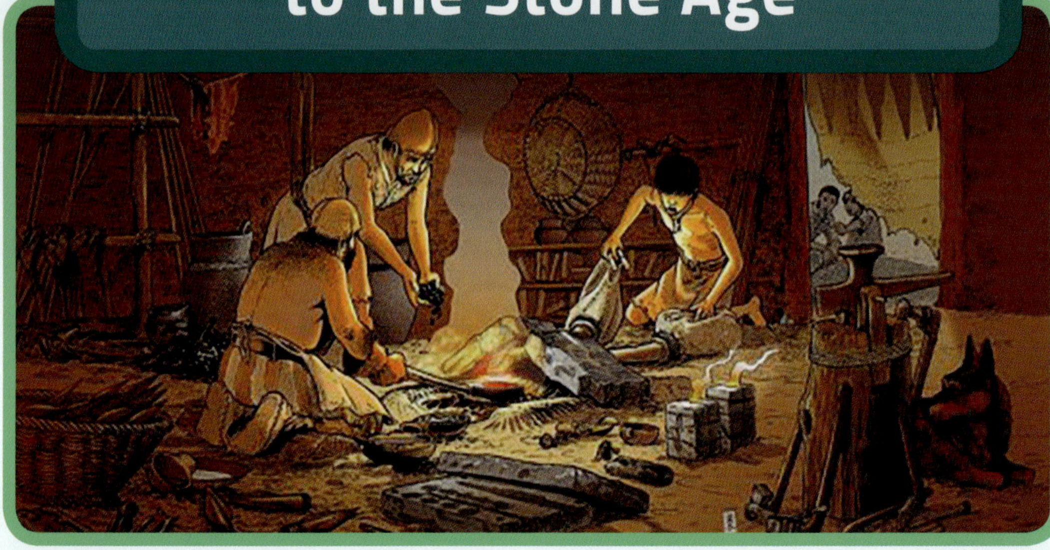

The Neolithic Era was the end of the Stone Age. The Stone Age lasted from 3.4 million years ago until 5,000 years ago. During that whole time, humans were using stone tools. But all that was about to change.

Neolithic people came up with a lot of great inventions. Eventually, these led to the use of metal instead of stone. This started a major transition for humankind. The transition period is called the Chalcolithic Era. Sometimes it's called the Copper Age. People during this time were performing copper metallurgy. Metallurgy means making something out of metal.

Working with metal requires really hot fires. They need to be hot enough to melt the metal. The metal can then be shaped into a weapon or a tool. Metal tools are better than stone tools. They can be made a lot sharper. They don't flake like stone tools do. They weigh less, so they're easier to carry around and use. As more people learned how to make metal tools, the Stone Age was left behind.

The Copper Age brought another hugely important invention. The wheel hit the scene. Wheels changed how humans lived, worked, and traveled.

The Neolithic era started with farming and staying in one place. But it ended with people about to go on the move.

14,500

Age in years of bread crumbs found in a desert in Jordan

- Archaeologists were excavating a Paleolithic house when they spotted the crumbs. This was in 2013.
- Before then, most researchers thought bread making began in the Neolithic era.
- Some discoveries answer questions. Others raise new questions.

Radiocarbon dating of the Ljubljana Marshes Wheel found in 2002 in Slovenai shows it is 5,150 years old.

Timeline of the Neolithic Era

The Neolithic Era – the New Stone Age – lasted from 9,000 years ago to 4,000 years ago.

9,000 years ago:
Farming takes off in southeast Asia.

9,000 years ago:
People in Çatalhöyük are creating elaborate figurines.

8,000 years ago:
With farming dominating the scene, people build larger permanent settlements.

7,000 years ago:
Conflict leaves farmers dead in Germany.

7,500 years ago:
Clay tokens are used for counting.

6,900 years ago:
People are building circular enclosures in central Europe.

6,000 years ago:
First copper tools are made.

5,500 years ago:
The wheel is invented.

A Neolithic stone axe with wooden handle still intact.

Glossary

agricultural
Related to farming.

archaeologist
Someone who studies ancient artifacts.

consensus
Agreement among all the people in a group.

devote
To spend a lot of time on.

disputed
Controversial. Something different people believe different things about.

domesticate
To turn wild animals into tamer ones; to grow a plant for human use.

enclosure
Something that fully surrounds an area, such as a fenced-in yard.

fertility
The ability to have children.

goods
Merchandise to sell or trade.

harvest
To gather food when it is ready to be eaten.

remains
The dead body of a person or animal; parts of something that are left when the rest is gone.

revolution
A major change that creates a new way of life.

Read More

Felix, Rebecca. *Unearthing Early Human Remains*. Minneapolis, MN: ABDO Publishing, 2019.

Ganeri, Anita. *Writing History: Stone Age*. London, UK: Franklin Watts, 2019.

Mooney, Carla. *Evolution: How Life Adapts to a Changing Environment.* River Junction, VT: Nomad Press, 2017.

Index

About the Author

Meg Marquardt started out as a scientist but likes writing about science even more. She enjoys researching physics, geology, and climate science. She lives in Madison, Wisconsin, with her two scientist cats, Lagrange and Doppler.